BRUSHED-OUT NECKLINE AND STARS--*easy to do using masking tape!*

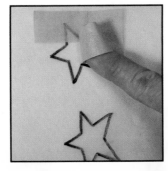

Brushed-out designs: Press masking tape firmly along one edge of the design. Squeeze a line of paint onto the tape near the edge. Use a stiff fabric paintbrush to pull the paint off the tape onto the fabric. Let dry, remove the tape, then squeeze a line of paint along the straight edge.

For stars (or other shapes): Use a pencil to trace the star shapes onto waxed paper. Apply masking tape strips side-by-side over the star; overlap the edges. Carefully pull the tape off as one piece, so the adhesive will pick up the pencil lines.

Cut out the tape star and place on the garment. Apply a thin bead of paint along the edges, then use the brush to pull it away from the tape. Pull off the tape. Optional: Squeeze a thin line of paint along the edges.

STAR SHIRT AND SHOES

For the shirt:
FS 201 white mist: one large star, one small star
FS 207 candy pink: one large star, two small stars
FS 214 golden blue: one large star, two small stars

For the shoes:
SC 352 pink glo: three stars
SC 353 green glo: two stars
SC 355 orange glo: two stars

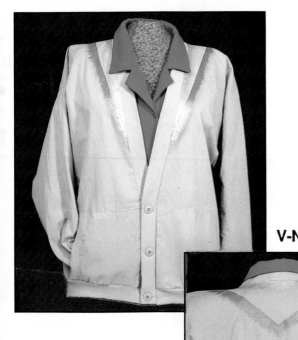

V-NECK JACKET

FS 217 seafoam green: inside lines
SC 217 seafoam green: line along the straight edge of the seafoam green area
FS 216 golden turquoise: outside lines
SC 216 golden turquoise: line along the straight edge of the turquoise area

STIPPLED DESIGNS--a "furry" look made with an *old* round fabric paintbrush

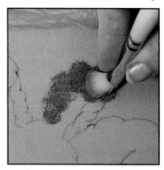

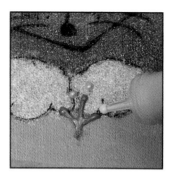

Dip the brush into paint and dab onto paper towels to remove half the paint.

With the brush perpendicular to the fabric, press down firmly--the bristles should spread. Repeat to fill the area.

Use the pen to go over the outlines and to draw the face. Paint the face, then squeeze on the eye and nose highlights and the flowers.

KITTEN NIGHTSHIRT
black fine line permanent pen: outlines, mouth, whiskers, eyelashes
FS 223 charcoal grey: body (except back paws and chest), head

FS 201 white mist: chest, back paws, eye whites, inner ears over grey

FS 139 black: nose, eye pupils, whisker dots

FS 215 shamrock green: eye irises

SC 207 candy pink: tongue, daisy petals

SC 204 gold mist: daisy centers

SC 214 golden blue: hyacinth petals

SC 217 seafoam green: stems and leaves

SC 110 white: eye and nose highlights

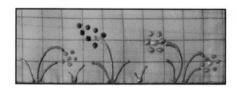

BUNNY DRESS
fine line permanent pen: outlines, whiskers, eyelashes

FS 222 golden brown: body (except inner ears, front paws, tail)

FS 201 white mist: inner ears, front paws, tail, eye whites

FS 139 black: nose, eye pupils, mouth, whisker dots

FS 207 candy pink: inner ears over white, cheeks over brown

SC 216 golden turquoise: flower stems, leaves

SC 207 candy pink: flower petals

SC 110 white: highlight nose & eyes

DRY-BRUSHED DESIGNS--*a simple, fail-proof way to paint, add shading, highlighting, or natural texture*

Dip the brush into paint and stroke on paper towels to remove most of the paint.

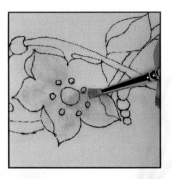

Lightly stroke the brush onto the fabric, allowing the background to show through.

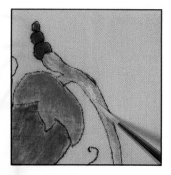

For shadows, dry-brush with a darker paint. For accents or highlights, dry-brush white paint on the design.

VINE JACKET
black fine line permanent pen: outlines
FS 113 butterscotch: top vine
FS 137 gingersnap: back vine
FS 123 lilac: light areas of blossoms and buds
FS 124 purple: dark areas of blossoms and flower buds; other bud balls at the ends of vines
FS 130 light turquoise: light areas of leaves
FS 131 deep turquoise: dark areas of leaves
FS 110 white: highlights on blossoms and leaves
SC 119 light pink: flower centers
SC 120 lipstick pink: dots around flower centers

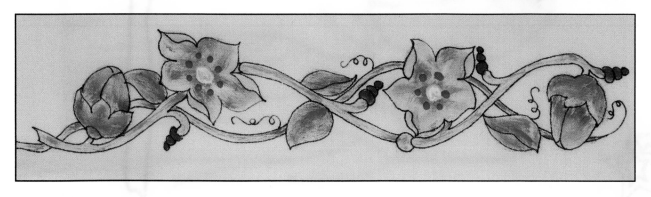

WATERCOLOR PAINTING--*mix each color with water to the consistency of light cream, then paint*

Transfer the pattern, then use the pen to outline the design. Use the lighter colors first, allowing the paint to "bleed" a little.

Carefully use the darker paints. Begin with small amounts, as more paint can be added if necessary.

If more highlights are desired, lightly brush on white paint.

BLUE ROSE SHIRT
black fine line permanent pen: outlines
FS 129 baby blue: light areas of blossoms
FS 128 medium blue: dark areas of blossoms
FS 136 chiffon green: light areas of leaves and stems
FS 132 evergreen: dark areas of leaves and stems
FS 201 white mist: extra highlights on flowers and leaves

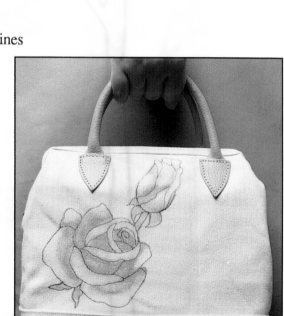

PINK ROSE SHIRT
black fine line permanent pen: outlines
FS 120 lipstick pink: dark areas of blossoms
FS 119 light pink: light areas of blossoms
FS 136 chiffon green: light areas of leaves and stems
FS 132 evergreen: dark areas of leaves and stems

LAVENDER ROSE PURSE
black fine line permanent pen: outlines
FS 123 lilac: light areas of blossoms
FS 124 purple: dark areas of blossoms
FS 136 chiffon green: stem and leaves
FS 201 white mist: extra highlights on flowers and leaves

test pattern

test pattern

test pattern

test pattern

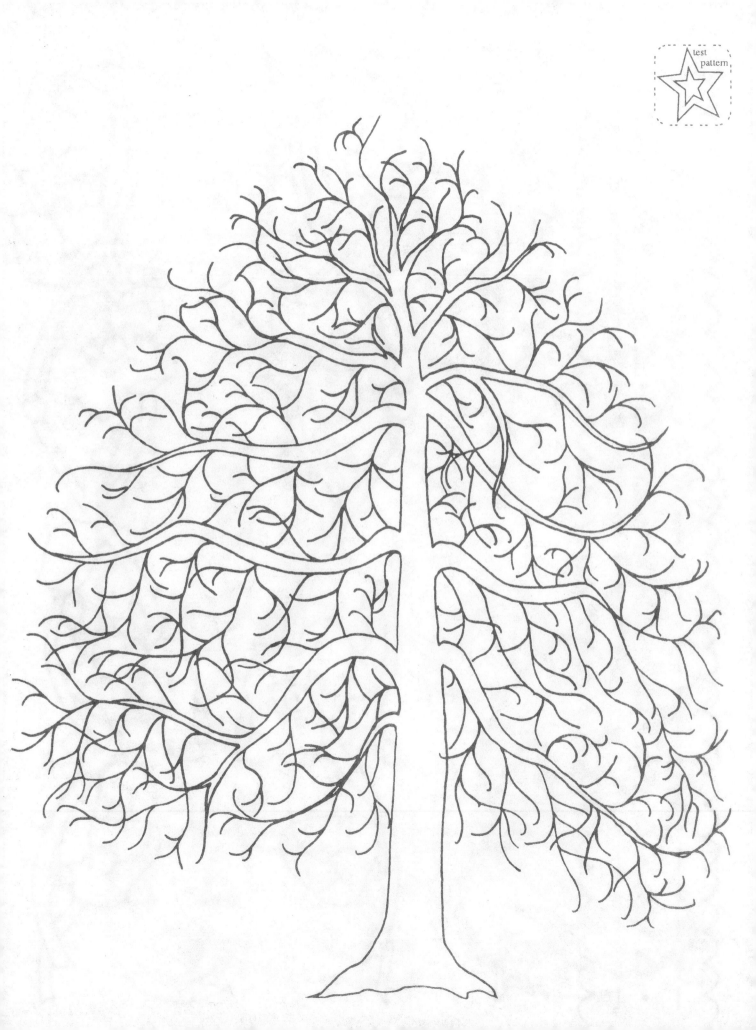

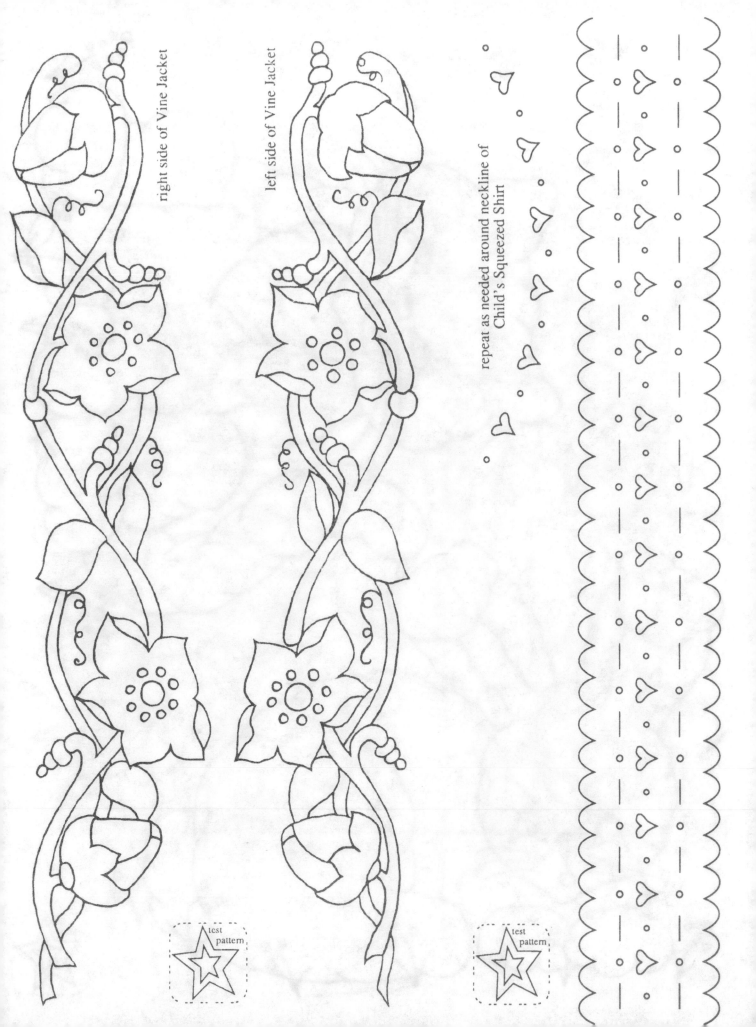

right side of Vine Jacket

left side of Vine Jacket

repeat as needed around neckline of
Child's Squeezed Shirt

test pattern

test pattern

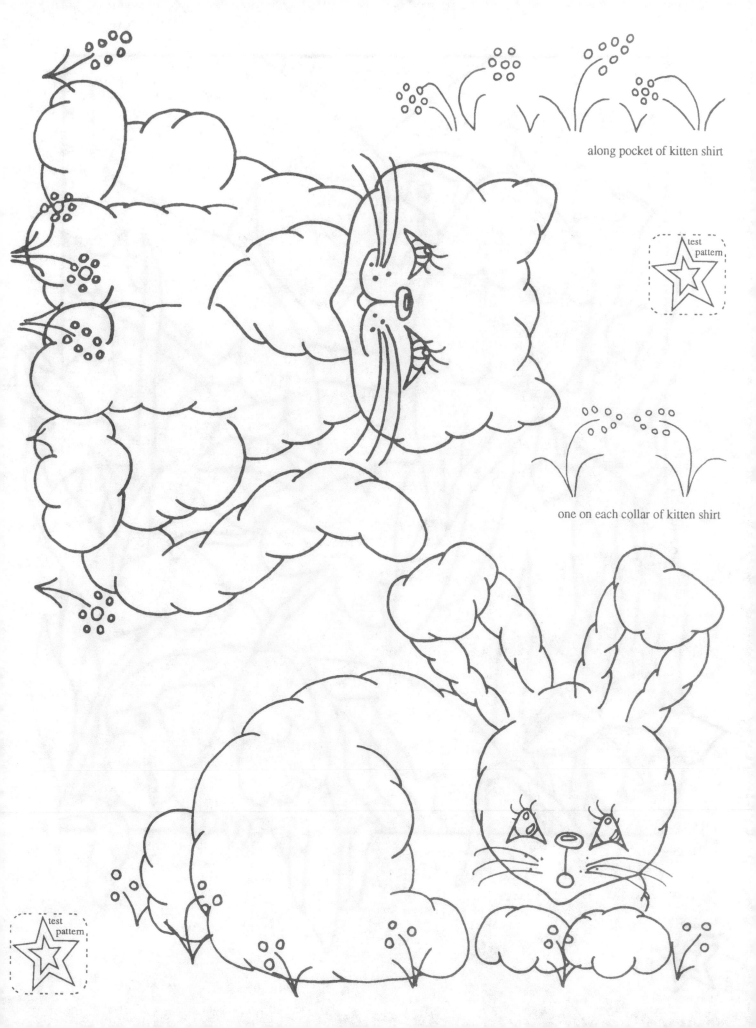

along pocket of kitten shirt

one on each collar of kitten shirt

"COLOR BOOK" PAINTING--*simplicity itself!*

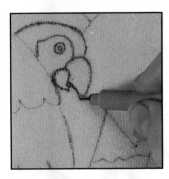

Transfer the pattern to the garment. Go over all lines with the pen.

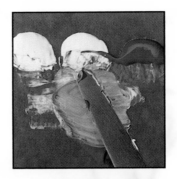

Squeeze each color onto a palette as you are ready to use it. This design calls for mixing two colors (2 parts white with 1 part evergreen): Squeeze out two drops of white and one drop of green onto your palette and mix with a palette knife. Recommended brushes: large areas with #6 flat, small sections with #2 round, and tiny or pointed areas with a liner.

For the eyes: Squeeze SC110 white to fill the eye areas. Wait a couple minutes, then carefully squeeze a tiny drop of SC 139 black for the pupil.

Two different jungle looks are achieved by simply changing the background color.

JUNGLE SHIRT
black fine line permanent pen: outlines
FS 132 evergreen: largest palm fronds
FS 133 Christmas green: grass-type leaves
FS 110 white (mix 2 parts white with 1 part evergreen): rounded leaves
FS 113 butterscotch: vines, stems
FS 137 gingersnap: large branches
FS 207 candy pink: flower outer petals
FS 209 watermelon: flower centers
FS 210 blush red: parrots' heads
FS 204 gold mist: parrots' faces
FS 206 apricot nectar: beaks, feet, lower parrot's neck
FS 214 golden blue: upper wings
FS 213 Holland blue: middle wings
FS 212 purple iris: lower wings
FS 216 golden turquoise: upper parrot's tail, lower parrot's breast
SC 110 white: eyes
SC 139 black: eye pupils; outline around frame

SPONGE-BLENDED DESIGNS--*this background is wonderful behind a silhouette!*

Cut a piece of paper to 8"x9". Position it on the shirt and apply two widths of masking tape just outside the edges. Discard the paper.

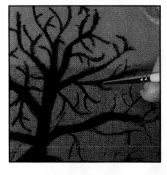

When the paint is dry, remove the tape. Transfer the tree pattern to the fabric, then use a #2 flat fabric brush for the trunk and a #00 round for the branches.

Dip a large round sponge brush into lipstick pink and dab along the lower 2" of the rectangle. Wash the brush, then dip into light pink and dab above the first band, making another 2" wide band and leaving 1" empty between the two bands.

Now mix equal parts lipstick pink with light pink and dab between the two bands. Paint the next band the lilac/purple mixture (see below), then mix it with light pink to paint the band between. Paint the last band blue, then mix blue with the lilac/purple to paint the band between.

SUNSET SHIRT
FS 120 lipstick pink: bottom band
FS 119 light pink: second band from the bottom
FS 123 lilac and FS 124 purple: mix 2 parts lilac with 1 part purple
   to sponge the third band from the bottom
FS 128 medium blue: top band
FS 139 black: tree; sponge lightly for ground

SHADING AND HIGHLIGHTING--*these techniques give depth to designs*

Shade items that are behind other items plus the edges of those that are in shadow. To shade: Use charcoal grey (or a darker shade of the same color) to paint shadows in the design.

Use white mist (or a lighter shade of the same color) to highlight areas that should "shine." Again, use very little paint in your brush, adding more strokes if needed. Use the pen to go over any paint-covered lines in the design.

GARDEN PURSE
black fine line permanent pen: outlines
FS 132 evergreen: tulip leaves
SC 132 evergreen: tulip stems
FS 209 watermelon: tulip blossoms
FS 218 golden green: daisy leaves
SC 218 golden green: daisy stems
FS 216 golden turquoise: daisy petals
FS 222 golden brown: daisy centers
FS 220 champagne ice: wheat
SC 220 champagne ice: frame
FS 223 charcoal grey: shading
FS 201 white mist: highlights

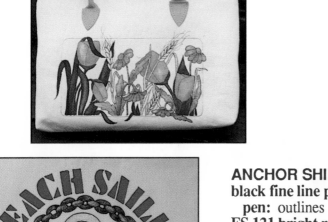

ANCHOR SHIRT
black fine line permanent pen: outlines
FS 121 bright red: letters
FS 126 bright blue: water
FS 125 navy: shade water
SC 301 glittering crystal: waves
FS 220 champagne ice: anchor
FS 223 charcoal grey: chains; mix with 2 parts champagne ice to shade the anchor
FS 137 gingersnap: anchor handle
FS 201 white mist: highlight water, anchor and chain
FS 139 black: shade chains; mix with 3 parts gingersnap to shade the anchor handle and make the wood grain lines

SQUEEZED AND STROKED DESIGNS--*just follow the lines!*

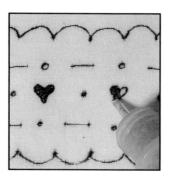

Squeezed: Shake the paint toward the bottle tip and squeeze a little onto a paper towel to eliminate air bubbles. When using, be sure the bottle tip touches the fabric.

To make each heart: Squeeze two comma shapes, then bring them together at the bottom.

Stroked: Pour out an "FS" color. Press a 1½" sponge or sponge brush into it, then onto the shirt. Pull down for 3-4 inches. Let one stroke dry before applying another; colors should overlap. Add random drips and lines of matching or contrasting "SC" colors.

CHILD'S SQUEEZED SHIRT AND BOOTIES

SC 307 glittering ruby: hearts
SC 305 glittering silver: straight lines
SC 311 glittering aquamarine: scalloped lines, dots

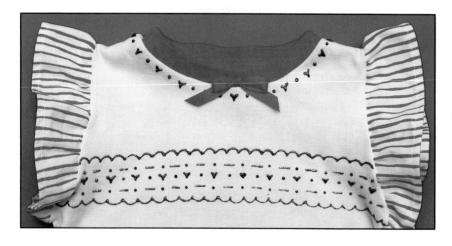

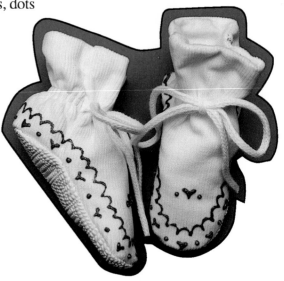

STROKED SHIRTS

FS 126 bright blue: strokes
FS 124 purple: strokes
FS 201 white mist: strokes

SC 126 bright blue: vertical lines, horizontal top lines on navy shirt
SC 124 purple: vertical lines, horizontal top lines on navy shirt
SC 201 white mist: vertical lines, horizontal top lines on navy shirt

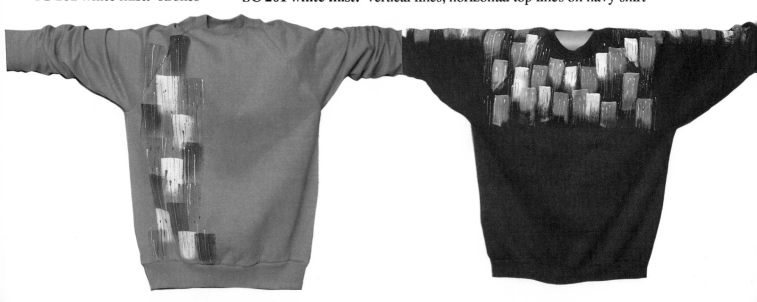